HANDWRITING *REVEALS YOU*
STROKES OF
UNCOMMON PERSONALITIES

Josh Batchelder, Graphologist

Contact: 770-621-9000, Fax 770-621-9521
Email: joshbatchelder@bellsouth.net
Mail: P.O. Box 450525, Atlanta, Georgia 31145

Trafford PUBLISHING® www.trafford.com

North America & international
toll-free: 844-688-6899 (USA & Canada)
fax: 812 355 4082

DEDICATION

To my father, John Thiery Batchelder, a loving teacher, by example, he taught me

about different occupations and acceptance of others.

FOREWARNED

Some of the characters you'll meet: In **Marry This Man?** we'll begin with a flamboyant, egotistical architect writing a note to a girl who showed it to me and asked me about the wisdom of dating him.

For contrast, we'll look behind a screen to see Becka's personality; she is a reticent talented librarian whose music is perfectly pleasing. Low-key in her dress and manner, she is unusual, a **Pearl in a Shell**!

Katy, in **Home Runs and Humor**, is a fun-loving paralegal, a people person. She is physically active and desires to be where the action is, whether it's hitting homers in softball games or involving herself in the office politics of a legal litigation firm.

Barbara in **Tear It Up and Start Again**, born into a circus family, presents a complete show of perfection in her precision and rhythm. Her unique combination of traits will provide a specimen that's worth studying.

Heather Worry Wort, newly married, is busy interacting socially and concerned with the here and now.

J. Henry in **A Strong West Wind** is "winging his way" through life full of energy, enthusiasm, impulsiveness and empathy. He has ventured far and wide and has an opinion on just about everything!

If you are not yet convinced that the handwritings of the above characters are distinctively different for good reason, in **We're all Different**, we'll visit a 5th grade classroom where we'll present samples from the forty-two students' cursive writings on "lined" paper stroking individual "Thank You" notes for a field trip to an air base. Despite intensive training in the Palmer method of handwriting you'll still observe different strokes, slants, heights, weightings, loops and margins that depart from the guidelines they are being taught to follow.

We all know that the world has sick people as well as healthy. In **Parking Lot Rage** you'll get a picture of a sarcastic, angry, paranoid specimen. Don W. entered the parking lot and penned intense venomous strokes on a windshield note to a patron who wasn't parked perfectly between the marked white lines. Was his rage due to deep unresolved feelings from past hurts?

Ruth Rigid, in **Caution, Careful...** is a medical administrator with numerous "hesitant" strokes throughout her unusual writing pattern. What does she reveal about her philosophical liberal/conservative views?

People form "strokes" with their writing instruments that are "accented" differently depending on the subject, person or situation they are writing to or about. Over time, they may change their "strokes" (personality traits) and give us a window, for example, to their degree of empathy, feelings, and defenses. To illustrate these changes, in **Head to Heart** we'll show you a three-time divorcee, Louise "The Squeeze." Early in her relationship with a widower friend she writes in a "cool headed" fashion. Ten months later we will see her more emotional "slant" as she pens a from-the-heart birthday note.

Jacob in **Real or Counterfeit** is an enigma. I have taken him out of the 19th Century world and examined his handwriting; I've explored his special talents. I've thought about the pressures of his family, work and money problems. His solution was the use of his special talents that landed him in a federal prison.

As I highlight these and other examples of intense traits (strokes), you will begin to look at the writings of others and your own to see the **real** persons' most prominent traits: We are using these unique strokes to help you see personalities through the window of writing, even though this will not be in a comprehensive, balanced way, as only the experienced analyst would. The trained handwriting analyst can organize and determine meaningful profiles that describe the subject's unique mental and emotional make-up without personally meeting the subject. So, the professional can comprehensively deal with historical figures, ancestors, loved ones and associates in a valid balanced way.

Let's have some fun as we examine the cast of characters chosen to help you gain more insight about your own circle. You'll come to appreciate their fine qualities. And, I'll prepare you for some out-of-balance personalities to help you recognize and deal with unpleasant or unexpected behaviors.

ABOUT THE AUTHOR

Josh Batchelder, CGA AB has performed professional handwriting services for over twenty-five years. He was trained and certified as a Graphoanalyst (C.G.A. 1976) by the International Graphoanalysts Society (Chicago, IL). He is a member of The Southern Handwriting Analysts Society (SHWAS), Columbia, S.C. Harvard College (AB 1959) Social Relations concentrating in social psychology, sociology, and small group dynamics.

His experience includes being analyst, author, teacher, and lecturer. Providing business and private handwriting analysis services. His focus has been personnel selection, comprehensive individual analyses, career cultivation reports, and business and personal compatibility studies.

Other Experience:

- Chartered Life Underwriter (CLU); Chartered Financial Consultant (ChFC).

- Atlanta Chapter Society, Society of Financial Service Professionals (21 years).

- Certified Toastmaster TM International.

- Northlake-DeKalb Kiwanis International (15 years) Programs

- U.S. Air Force Lt/Colonel (Retired) combined 5000 flying hours as Radar Jet Intercept Officer; Worldwide Airlift Missions as Chief Wing Navigator;

- Civil Air Patrol Pilot (instrument rated) and Aerospace Education Officer for Peachtree DeKalb Squadron Georgia Wing.

- Program Coordinator for several church groups and the Civil Air Patrol.

Married, with adult children and grandchildren. Other attachments include Shelly a female miniature Schnauzer.

TABLE OF CONTENTS

CONTENTS

INTRODUCTION

The idea for this book emanated largely from a series of "on-board" lectures performed for three major cruise lines. Abbreviated profiles of my most unusual personalities' writing stroke specimens were used to identify their talents, character flaws, or compatibility questions.

From the hundreds of handwriting specimens I have examined over the past quarter century, I have selected samples from individuals around the world that exhibit standout character traits. These traits, evident in their exaggerated handwriting "strokes", most everyone would easily observe and say wow! And their loved ones and friends would agree, "yes that's Jim or Jane alright!" Highlighting these uncommon strokes is a way for the average person to gain insight; and, easily remember what personality traits are represented by these strokes; especially when they have their equivalent meanings in body language.
My objective is not to answer why or how these people write as they do, but to illustrate how handwriting analysis allows us to view the dominant traits of a person's emotional and mental make up and processes. Perhaps you my reader will discover some of these traits in your own less exaggerated handwriting strokes; for many professional analysts conclude that exaggerated stokes are a negative.

The neuromuscular projections found in our handwriting strokes (including those in our signatures),[1] are loaded with information that can give us a comprehensive view of complex personality patterns. For example, the efficiency of our mental processes can be enhanced by some traits and impeded by other traits.

---

[1]

Writers' signatures represent how they want to be viewed by others; whereas the body of cursive writing generally is the real person. In many respects, most signatures are different than the body of cursive writing.

ENHANCING TRAITS	IMPEDING TRAITS
Optimism	Procrastination
Directness	Resentments
Fluidity	Self-consciousness
Concentration	Paranoia
Loyalty	Pessimism
Rhythm	Prejudice
Organizational Ability	Repression
Intuitiveness	Self-deceit
Attention to details	Impulsiveness
Broad-mindedness	Confusion of Interest
Independent Thinking	Inattention to details
Honesty	Dishonesty
	Indecision

These profiles will be answering many of the questions about what we can or cannot see in handwriting. And I will illustrate in several profiles how our writing changes as we change.

Many people, upon my first meeting them, feel exposed because I demonstrate how swiftly I can tell them about their dominant traits from their short handwriting samples.

My children have never asked me how I thought they were doing **except** when they gave me their handwriting samples. My surprise was they accepted my advice from the traits I indicated in their writing. For example, many children and adults have no intermediate or long-term goals; that absence affects their ability to achieve. Another example, many young people are very self-conscious; this gets in the way of their achieving goals. I can remind them to relax, because others are not looking at them critically, for they are too busy looking at themselves.

Though basic compatibility in business and personal relationships can be determined from handwritings, common culture and common values play a big part in how well people can function together, even if a number of their traits may indicate incompatibility.

I'm continually impressed with how different from each other we all are, even within the same family. Once we begin thinking about and treating others as individuals, we likely will cease expecting them to think and act as we do. Handwriting analysis helps us by comprehensively displaying personality traits and their dominant resulting forces thereby helping us to appreciate and accept another human being's uniqueness.

In this work I will present snapshots of prominent personality traits - not complete or comprehensive - analyses. There will be some interesting revelations surrounding many of these specimens. I will also answer many of the common questions people ask during my lectures, demonstrations and teaching. For example:

1. Can we tell whether it's a man or woman's handwriting?
2. Does our handwriting change as we change?
3. What do signatures tell us?
4. Can we change our personality by changing our handwriting "habits"?
5. What about people who print?
6. What can we learn from a person's handwriting?
7. Why do people's handwriting vary from the way they were taught to write?

ACKNOWLEDGEMENTS

Where did it begin? With my father John Thiery Batchelder, Boston attorney, who was my live model for 15 years. He taught me tolerance, understanding, and love. His bedtime stories was a series that went on and on about Robert Morely's job changes. These escapades sparked my fascination with people's occupations.

My mother, Emma Macaulay Batchelder, who taught me the warmth of family gatherings around the dinner table. Always providing tasty and healthy eating, she encouraged an appreciation for good health habits and industry.

My wife, Betty Ann Sage, playing Vanna White during our cruise lectures. Betty Ann listened to my words and often found better ways to describe my characters without changing their essential traits. She accepted my spending many hours in my "cave" to reflect and write.

My favorite sister, Nancy Elizabeth Sephton, Berkeley, California. She was my cheering section and enthusiastic chief of editing. She insists she loves fixing my numerous writing errors. Still, she reminded me to go with my "gut" whenever in doubt. So, any mistakes are probably from rewrites I didn't forward for her review.

Emilie Stockholm my instructor throughout several years of IGAS (International Graphoanalysis Society) training for certification. She guided me toward more professional analyses.

Audrey Dixon of Dixon's Word Processing blessed many hours with labor and laughter as we looked at with behind the scenes stories about my specimens. She suffered decoding my crammed writing strokes and then patiently performed rewrites ...so many I believe she has learned the subject well enough to be certified. Her creative touches and comments often helped me to settle on the sounds and words I wanted to convey. Growing up in Jamaica and learning the "King's English" and having a broad cultural background contributed mightily to moving this book along. She's a "keeper" for my next book.

Robert Coram, Atlanta author of some dozen novels and non-fiction works including a 2002 book about John Boyd – the fighter pilot who changed the art of war. His generous and kind critique about the **real world** for new authors helped me rethink my approach to agents and publishers.

Catherine Lane, President of the Florida Chapter of Handwriting Analysts for her comments. Ann Miraglio, Master Graphoanalyst and 1997 IGAS Analyst of the Year for her input; Eileen Page, MA and Master Graphoanalyst, Author, Teacher and Lecturer for her excellent lectures, books and comments about my writing efforts.

Janet Tilden, recent Dean of Instruction for IGAS (International Graphoanalysts Society) gave me added perspective about this book.

Last, but certainly not the least, my many friends of the Southern Handwriting Analysts Society (SHWAS), Columbia, South Carolina, vetted a number of my interpretations of extraordinary subjects.

SUBJECT #1

SUBJECT 1
MARRY THIS MAN? - (Mr. "X")

Pat, a young executive assistant asks about dating Mr. "X". He's a flamboyant successful architect. He lives an exciting life of travel, consulting and designing inspiring edifices. My analysis: He possesses, in spades, all the talent needed for success in his unique specialization. Huge **ego** shows in the large letters[1]; **will power**, in the heavy t-crossbars; and **imagination** in his high above-the-baseline loops. Note his l's, h's, and t's. His **rhythm, determination, directness**, and **showmanship** are other traits that help him create his imaginative designs. You will see showmanship in the embellishments of his stroke markings.

His contagious **enthusiasm**[2] (evident in the long t-crossbars) will persuade clients to buy his concepts and plans. He's an **imaginative** soul (it's in-the-loops) as seen in l's, t's (the work area of ones life); however, these loops in t's also mean that he's likely to be easily offended (i.e., **paranoia**) by criticism of his work; and the loops in d's (the personal side of his life). This means that his imagination takes comments about his person far beyond any well-meaning remarks.

In another aspect, his highly penetrating strokes (above the baseline) indicate a continual search for "new" material (questions, concepts and rich experiences) to enhance his work. **Self-reliance** (doubly so) is in two underlinings, is <u>very great</u>; and **determination** is evident in the lengthy straight down strokes in his 'y's. There are other traits, like excellent **rhythm**[3] (consistent spacing between his letters and words), and, an "ace" for any person, his **intuition** seen in his word "totally" (breaks between letters). Now that we've proved he must be very successful, professionally; what will guarantee he's a comfortable compatible companion for our young executive assistant, Pat?

Pat's friend charges out-of-the-gate-like-a-bull; Pat had better be strong enough to "cage" this heavy, intense creature that harbors many deep feelings. Don't count on them fading fast either (see the heavy down pressure[4] in his writing strokes). This means that all sensory experience will remain for a long time. So, one sunny

---

[1]   See Appendix D **size of writing**.
[2]   See Appendix F **"T" strokes.**
[3]   See Appendix D **rhythm.**
[4]   See Appendix D – **pressure/depth of sensory experiences.**

day you're riding down the coast with him and some sight, sound, or smell reminds him of a negative interpersonal event. Don't be surprised if an angry outburst occurs. How do we know this? Well, his most common slant of "strokes", up to 30% right of vertical, represent **unexpressed feelings** which can accumulate until they reach the breaking point, like a dam that breaks! So, if it's anger, watch out! Even though his larger writing indicates a mostly **gregarious** personality.

So, Pat has a man whose **high goals** are all achievable (the t-crossbars are all on his t-stems). He has **high energy** [5] and the combination of traits that would place him above most in his profession. Now, notice where he wills that they "someday meet totally" with heavier t-crossbar (remember will power) than the other t-crossbars. Here's an example of added emphasis coming out stronger than his other strong willed t-crossbars. Very few companions could ever expect to do anything but yield to this overpowering personality. Consequently, I told **Pat** you must decide if you're willing to support and yield to this never dull man in return for the likely expansive life of luxury surrounded by distinctive designs of inspiring spiritual edifices. Keeping him as an exciting interesting friend may be a much safer option.

This is a good example of an instances where I advise my clients to stand back and observe behavior of their "intended" amongst family, friends and colleagues; because over a period of a year or two your intended's behavior with others will be what you will experience too.

---

[5]   See Appendix D – **size of writing.**

Now is the time for all good men to come to the aid of their country.

May the Lord bless you and keep you. The Lord make His face to shine upon you. The Lord lift up His countenance upon you, and give you peace.

6/95   Beck

Subject #2 specimens

Mr. Joshua Botchelder
P. O. Box 450525
Atlanta, Georgia 31145 - 0525

145/0525 |..||...||...||.|.|.|||.||.|.|..||..|.|.||.|.|.||

SUBJECT 2
PEARL IN A SHELL!
- (Becka)

Writing doesn't come much smaller than Becka's and still be readable. You may want to get out your magnifying glass to examine her "strokes" as I talk about them. She is very demure person.

It's rare that you will see such micro strokes[6] formed with such **precision**, and exceptional **manual dexterity**. Notice her **rhythm** in the very even spacing between the letters and words. **Attention to details** shows in her dotted i's and crossed t's. The very small writing, as though done with a laser beam, intensifies all her other traits including **memory**, **intelligence**, and **loyalty** (rounded "I" dots).

My curiosity to explore Becka's talents, and any major changes in her life of the past seven years, prompted me to call the church to make contact. I learned about her life and work; and how her personality traits suit her professional work and volunteer activities. Great **concentration** is seen in the very small strokes or letters we often see in the scientists, researchers, and accountants. Conversely, large letters are associated with gregarious persons. **Reticence** is evidenced in the closed strokes especially seen in a's and o's. **Caution** is found in the straight final stroke endings in Becka's words. Her traits form the perfect combination for her work as a librarian.

Since her upstrokes remain close to the baseline, she shows no significant **exploration** of the **philosophical/theoretical** areas, and by her downstrokes being close to the baseline very little room for outside exploration of other persons and places. Therefore her world is very much **in the present**, confined to the business of her family, work and her selective social circles. She does not explore outside of her well-defined world.

Piano playing and recitals were part of her early history growing up in a small Southern town where both parents were practicing attorneys. Upon entering a major university in a big city she majored in political science and ceased her piano playing. Her musical interests were restarted with singing in the church choir. In recent years her piano skills were called upon to play for church services. Several years ago a professional musician noticed her extraordinary skills and persuaded her to join him in playing piano and organ duets for the church. I accepted an invitation to an evening program of music and witnessed a stellar performance. She and her colleague performed a medley of Bach,

---

[6]   Appendix D – **micro size**

Mozart and Beethoven that was totally thrilling. It confirmed my analysis of talents seen in her writing.

The **signature** is one's most practiced expression of how one wishes to be perceived by the public. Looking at Becka's signature, which is very much like the body of her writing; she's unlike most people. That is, she **represents herself** exactly as she is (signature strokes are not different from her other writing). Becka's dress and make-up at that Wednesday evening program were plain and unaffected. It fit her **reserved personality** (very small writing); she didn't seem to want to attract attention. In contrast, her male colleague's demeanor was outgoing and enthusiastic. He led with passionate musical expression, deflecting attention from her great performance; Becka would just as soon slip out the side door after her performance.

Now more questions: How did her teachers react to her very small writing. What was the impact of her being an only child of two attorneys in a small town? What character traits will be modified from her contact with the church members, and others who are beginning to recognize her exceptional musical talent. Yes, she's a PEARL IN A SHELL and here is a good example of how handwriting analysis revealed Becka's beauty within.

SUBJECT 3
HOME RUNS AND HUMOR – (KATY)

When I show you Katy's "strokes" you'll understand why she quit working in a small life insurance sales and service office. Look at the big "p" loops. They tell us that she prefers to be where the action is rather than being a spectator. A **gregarious** (larger letter forms) **fun loving** young woman with a flowery **sense of humor** (bending initial strokes seen in the words "might", "but", and "have"). In fact, when she was in the hospital, I bought her three "get well" cards because I could easily envision her laughing at all three cards. She has capacity for many friends (big loops in "y's"). Active physically, she could hit multiple homers for her girls' softball team. Manual dexterity showed in her squared r's, good **rhythm** or timing to hit those homers (even spacing of letters and words). **Intuition** (breaks in letters after first two) helps her "read" others well. **Gregariousness** was evident in her large writing strokes.

Two areas can reduce her effectiveness; capacity for **resentment** (seen in stiff initial strokes beginning below the baseline, some examples in the words "want", "wanted", "re", "suggestions", "say", and "what"). In spite of her sense of humor, the frequency and the intensity of her **resentment** strokes are unusual. Katy's **procrastination** (seen in "t" crossbars that stop at stem) plagued her efforts to finish projects. She had the quick **understanding** (needle points on her "r's") and **determination** to carry things out (straight down strokes on y's). Her fun loving sense of humor and smile will likely overcome any boss' irritation over her procrastination. Now you know why she quit insurance in favor of the excitement, action and camaraderie of a litigating legal firm.

Joshua —
You might want to re-arrange
Section VI - Suggestions - I knew
what I wanted to say, but didn't
have time to say it properly -

The path goes from place to place
With no time and throughout all space.
It goes from mountain top to valley low.
It goes very fast or very slow.
It leads out from planet to planet.
It is not tangible to those who would plan it.
It goes back and forth from space
and God to man
and back again.

SUBJECT 4
TEAR IT UP AND START AGAIN - Barbara

Barbara's writing shows all of the major marks of a "top flight" performer except the **confusion** of having too many "irons-in-the-fire" at the same time (see the numerous strokes that strike other strokes in other lines).

Could she have performed well in the circus as a gymnast, or high wire performer? She prefers being **physically in the action** (loops in her p's). The extended depth in down strokes and the height of upstrokes show **desire for new experiences and change**. **Artistry** and **manual dexterity** are found in her squared r's, along with **precision** in the formation of her letters. Great **rhythm** is evident in the consistent even spacing between letters and words. And a very **steady** person (you can put a ruler on her baseline and see that it's moderately straight). Here is a sign she's emotionally well-balanced.

Barbara's got a strong **desire to be unique** (seen in her circled i-dots). While she has this drive to be seen as unique and with a bit of showmanship, embellishment of strokes (seen in her I's and T's), she still is very **self-conscious** (note the elevated last humps on her m's and n's "sticking out" higher). Did her physical attributes account for her preoccupation with noticing herself too much? She was short, round-figured and very well-endowed; a rounded face with full curly black hair, a gypsy appearance not often seen.

She'd worked some years for an accounting firm; and I'm sure her rhythm precision and **steady emotional nature** was valued. Subsequently she worked for a small life insurance sales office as "Girl Friday" who had to do a variety of tasks, including taking phone calls, typing, calculating and starting projects, and stopping some projects going nowhere.

Barbara possessed so many exceptional traits, not evident from a casual look at her persona. Here is an example of how handwriting analysis can go behind a facade to see a person's talents. She possessed **literary talent** (her Greek e's), **artistic** utility in her squared r's: **Intuition** in the frequent breaks in her letters, (it's like stopping to let insight enter). **Vanity** shows in her very high (3 ½ times height of case letters) stems. Great **organizational skills** are seen in her balanced loops. **Honesty** in clear o's and a's and **directness** in frequent T's without initial up strokes.

One evening her boss returned to the office and noticed a wastebasket full of "crumpled" typing paper. This was the mid-70's when word processing wasn't prevalent. Upon examining the "crumpled" paper her boss discovered a number of minor errors. Barbara "started over" after each error until the letter was perfect. She couldn't stand seeing a performance that wasn't done perfectly! I concluded that Barbara did not really enjoy the frequent and varied activities experienced in her small sales office. Like a circus act, she would prefer performing integrated, completed tasks that would satisfy her desire to have near perfect performances fully utilizing her combination of exceptional talents.

Next God Damn time you park tell me and I'll stay out of park lot since they mean nothing you stupid Son of a Bitch

SUBJECT 5
PARKING LOT RAGE - (Don W.)

Feel the rage when you look at this man's writing strokes. Imagine his body language - it sticks out. So much so he is even **self-conscious** about his own behavior (notice the last hump in the "m" in "me" evident in the last hump above the first in his "m" and "n's"). **Sarcasm** is in his barbed t-bar endings.

In a hurry, I parked poorly on the white lines in a mall parking lot. Don W. entered the scene, and attacked me with his penned venomous strokes on a note stuck to my windshield, my most prized specimen! His writing strokes so perfectly fit his message! And since he was so public, I present it for your viewing. Loops in his "p's" tells us he prefers to be **physically** down on the field playing. **Depth** of his feelings you experience with the heavy down pressure of his strokes. All of the **senses** he experiences (sight, smell, touch, hearing and taste) will be everlasting! Heavy t-bars show his **will power**. His **enthusiasm** and **enduring-energy** are in the long t-bars. **Paranoia** is present in the big loops in his d-stems (personal area) and in his t-stems (work area). So, **don't comment** on his person or his work!! **Deep resentment**, notice his body language; it's in his long straight upstrokes in the word 'since'. Irregular, faded and heavy writing often are seen in sick people. **Egotistical** behavior can be expected from the person who writes with very large letters. All-in-all, an **impulsive**, explosive, **angry** man. He's dangerous; remember he jumped out of his vehicle to write a note to express his hate and sign his full name.

V Doug !!!!!!

3-20-01

I wanted you to have this block as a symbol of the way I would like our Re lationship to be built — ONE Block at a time for a sturdy foundation — Not to be torn down. Everything needs a strong foundation. Understand ?? no. 3/20/01

SubJecT 6

Doug,

Just think it will soon be a year + you have meant so much to me.

2/02

2/02

SUBJECT 6
HEAD TO HEART – (LOUISE, THE SQUEEZE)

Louise in her mid 50's coming from three previous marriages writes to a widower, Doug. Early in this relationship, her upstrokes (vertical slant) indicated that she approached her friendship with her head. Was she trying to avoid any mistakes of getting into a new relationship, not moving **impulsively** or **expressing** too many **feelings**; or, was she moving carefully so as not to scare her friend who had come from one marriage of many long years? Some other traits Louise brought to her dealings with others: She was very **sensitive to criticism** of her work (big loops in her "t's") and her person (d-loops).

The margins to the left of her writing are very wide showing **isolation from her past** (herself, family?) and some **distancing with the future/others** is in the wide right margin. She was inclined to be **direct** (no upstroke in "T's").

The loops in her "p's" mean she prefers to be **physically active**. The intersecting of her strokes with lines above and below tells us she has many irons in the fire. She has to be very active in business with many friends; the loops in her "y's" show **imagination**, allowing for many friends.

Ten months later Louise wrote a note on birthday card to Doug. Notice also the left margin was quite narrow showing the change to more comfort with self and past (and need for **security** in her surroundings). Her continued wide right margins could mean she was still quite hesitant with leaping into the future. Her "slant" on things is now very different (65 degree slant in her far right strokes). Her right slanted upstrokes indicated more **emotional expression of feelings** and **impulsiveness**.

Now, **it's gone from her head to heart**.

hi Joshua and Bettyann
Hope this card finds
you well and hope
you like these pictures.
It was a real pleasure
meeting you both. We
hope to cross paths again
one day soon. Have a
safe journey to bermuda.
Take Care
♡ Matthew & Enola

SUBJECT #7

SUBJECT 7
HEATHER WORRY WORT! – (Heather)

A youthful, gregarious pixie living very much in the present (middle zone strokes) using her imagination (where in "m's" and "n's" you see loops) to **worry** over most anything every minute except **philosophical, spiritual** or **theoretical** matters (no stroke penetration above the middle zone). She can accumulate many friends (loops in her "y's" and again in word "journey"*)

Driving her to lead the conversation for herself and her husband is her great need to communicate (nearly no margins); this also is indicative of insecurity often found in younger people. Other traits associated with no margins are very frugal persons and busybodies**.

Heather is newly married and struggling to establish her identity and direction. She has not set any long term goals (t-bars on her consonants). Heather is physically active (seen in p-loops). For some reason she has some resentments (see the stiff upstrokes that start below the baseline at the beginning of words: "Real", "to", and "there").

Overall, a beautiful, chatty, gregarious young lady who is certain to be into all of the details (she dots all her "i's" and crosses her "t's") of everyday conversation and up for plenty of physical activity.

---

*While certain strokes/traits occur most often within particular letters, they can occur elsewhere with the same meaning.

**Mary Metzler <u>Margins</u> revised edition 1981

SUBJECT 8

1976

Now is the time for all you
to come to the aid of their party.
My favorite hobby is flying
four seasons and four fortunes

4/03

Now is the time for all good men
and women to come to the aid
of their country

4/03

SUBJECT 8
A STRONG WEST WIND - (J. Henry)

Time changes us; and here's two specimens that (over 27 years) will illustrate J. Henry's clear shift away from very far forward (right slanted upstrokes) that are present in impulsive more opinionated people (those inclined to express their feelings if other traits don't restrict their expression). You can feel the constant (no change in slant) strong rightward leaning strokes in specimen #1. Other traits presented here are **directness** (no upstroke on "T's"), **enthusiasm** and **energy** (long t-bars). **Organization** (balanced f-loops) and **rhythm** (even space between letters and words) plus **will power** (down pressure t-bars) and **determination** (straight long downstrokes on "y") helped this character accomplish much in spite of his being **impulsive** and **opinionated** (like many actors able to express their emotions). Far forward slanted writing also is a stroke/trait, which indicates capacity to **empathize** with others.

Thirty-seven years later in specimen #2, the strong west wind is less intense, yet steady (a whole quadrant of consistently less right leaning strokes).

Also, the t-bars were much shorter (less enthusiasm and energy expended). Though time and experiences have changed J. Henry's traits, many didn't change: for example, his **optimism** (baselines slanted up), **upbeat** attitude (upward slanted t-bars in "the", "time", and "their"); also **determination** (downstrokes in "y's") remained strong. Many other traits are evident that contributed to J. Henry's success and happiness but they aren't necessary to illustrate how our writing strokes/traits change as we change*.

---

*Graphotherapy is that discipline that seeks to change behavior by changing behavioral traits through the exercise of changing stroke habits. It is also possible to change our personality traits by changing our writing strokes.

Subjects 9A through 9P
WE'RE ALL DIFFERENT

Thirty-seven years ago in the middle of intensive Palmer Method of Handwriting Training 42 fifth grade classmates penned "thank you" notes to me for a field trip to Dobbins Air Force Base in Georgia. The trip was a big success; the students were enthusiastic and into their individually different comments.* Despite the student's use of lined paper that set the desired standard size strokes, margins, and heights of letters you will witness how unique each student's strokes were with the different slants and downward writing pressures. Some 15% will write with near vertical slant (**objectivity**) and perhaps 5% leftward slant (**withdrawal** sign); some 80% will have varying degrees of rightward slanted upstrokes (more **impulsive** and inclined to **express feelings**). Many young people have **low self-esteem** as they have not set goals in life (see low t-bars on stems). I believe it is generally accepted that having goals these young people will make better decisions; and thus they will have more purpose in their lives and feel better about themselves.

You'll see different heights in the "bars" high or low on t-stems that represent longer or shorter-range **goals**, respectively. If you look first at the whole writing sample to sense the "**body language**" or prevailing style of the subject before you read about the prominent traits of the selected subjects, you will be able to better understand the overall personality picture.

---

*Getting handwriting specimens that are natural to the writer, that do not require lots of thought, helps to obtain a truer sample of their personality. We will get these better samples when the writer doesn't know that the writing is going to be analyzed or when they are writing to a loved one or friend or writing about a familiar subject.

1443 Iroquois Path
Atlanta 19, Ga.
April 21, 1966

Dear Major Batchelder,
    I would like to thank you for taking us through Dobbins Air Force Base. I thought going through the M.A.T. airplane was fun and interesting. I want to thank you for telling us how you fly to Viet Nam, too. It was fun getting out of school, too.

Sincerely,
Bill Barrington

SUBJECT 9A
ART APTITUDE - Bill Barrington

Bill B, an **enthusiastic** young man (long t-crossbars) with good **organizational skills** (balanced f-loops). **Loyalty** is his strong suit (solid rounded i-dots). Bill is inclined to **hang onto the security of the past** (very narrow left margins*) and very **hesitant** to move ahead (security need); also his widening right margins indicate further hesitation to leap into the future. Thus, I conclude he is a homebody. A **nurturing spirit toward others** (see cupping base stroke of capital "I" and his very slanted "right" upstrokes, 45 degrees plus indicating **empathy** with others).

The clear, heavier* precise writing strokes and good **rhythm** (spacing of letters and words) are indicative of an artistic personality. Clear heavy lines also are present in those with those with a rich **color sense** and **line appreciation**. In addition he had excellent **manual dexterity** (squared r's). These artistic traits helped Bill to have an unusual appreciation of his surroundings and the art world. His artistic talents were available to him whether or not his main occupation was that of an artist.

Exploration of his world is seen in the extension of his up and down strokes; which also indicate a need for new experiences, which he would have engaged in enthusiastically (long t-bars).

Some personal asides of where young Bill was 37 years ago: **Procrastination** was evident (note the t-crossbars not fully finished after the stem); with all of his many talents, enthusiasm and **exploration**, etc. and his desire to utilize all of his interests, it is no wonder that some procrastination to accomplish everything would be present. Also Bill was somewhat **self-conscious** (note the last higher hump of letters "m" or "n"). At age 11, self-consciousness is common.

He had an excellent relationship with both parents (seen in fully-balanced capital "I" upper and lower loops). Think about this; how often have we seen such an extraordinary 11-year-old as Bill?

---

*The sample of the 37-year-old writing shows lighter down pressure than was present when written.

Love,

Libbet

Jones

4977 Mill Creek Ro

Atlanta, Georgia

April 21, 1966

Dear Major Batchelder,

Our class would very much to Thank you for our wonderful field trip. I think our class liked the simulator the best. We liked the tower too. We enjoyed looking through one of the planes too. I am sure we have got some pictures to remember of the interesting day at Dobbins Air Force Base

SUBJECT 9B
LOVE EXPRESSED - LIBBET, J.

Libbet was a loving young girl (very rounded writing) **expressing love** for others (prevailing right slant of upstrokes, over 45 degrees). Her very weak **energy** and **will power** to accomplish work (shows in her short and light down pressure of t-bars) respectively; this also means she is short of **enthusiasm** (short t-bars). An **independent** streak is seen in her proportionately short d-stems. Therefore she would not have been keen to share personal activity. Libby's **temper** shows up occasionally when we see her t-bars begin right of the stem (see "Atlanta", "Batchelder", "trip", "the", "pictures", and "interesting"). She also shows a tendency toward **selfishness** in the curled initial loops of her capital letters (see "Mill Creek" and "major"); however, she has a tendency to **seek responsibility** (notice in the word "thank" the much larger loop back to the left). Now take this trait and combine it with her **nurturing** side (the cupped lower loop on her capital "I's" and on "T's" in the word "Thank") and you will understand how she would volunteer for group activities that will satisfy her own objectives.

You will notice throughout the specimens how often the message of the writer fits the traits. For example, Libbet is one of the few students who signed her letter "love" (inset signature page). Now remember subject #5 Don W's note of rage fit all of his angry traits. An exception is Subject #18 Ms. Nasty Nice whose message is hiding her underlying temper observed in the strokes. She was hiding her real feelings.

SUBJECT R

3434 Ashford Dunwoody Road
Atlanta 19, Georgia 30319
April 21, 1966

Dear Major Batchelder,

I would like to thank you for taking us through Robbins Air Force Base. I especially enjoyed the flight simulator and M.A.T.S. Its too bad they didn't have any power in the controll room when we were there.

Yours truly,
Jeff Lewis

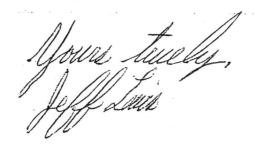

what to

SUBJECT 9C
THE PHILOSOPHER - JEFF L.

Jeff L. **related well** to others (very right slanted upstrokes commonly 60 degrees off vertical*) with a strong **desire for change** and **variety** (penetration well into the upper zone on his upstrokes). **Emotional memory** of sensory experiences was short lived (he had light down pressure in his writing). Also the **energy** level he expended to accomplish goals was short-lived (short t-bars). His narrow left margin meant that he was inclined to hang onto the past (**security** need in narrow left margin) and avoid leaping into the future (wide right margin). His letter "h"[7] represented his capacity for success; and his high "h" upstrokes indicated a strong need for **new experiences** in this realm. Also Metzler explains in her book that the letter "l" relates to ones **intellectual imagination, ethics,** and **personal philosophy.** The loops in Jeff's "p's" showed his interest in being **physically very active.** His **organizational** skills were exemplary (very balanced f-loops). His **goals** were all practical (t-bars on the stem). Jeff was not long on **enthusiasm** (short t-bars) or the application of **will power,** which is shown in the light depth of his t-bars, and his short t-bars also meant that his energy was only available for short spurts. **Rhythm** available to him was excellent (even spacing of words and letters).

All of these traits helped me to appreciate what a classmate said January 20th, 2003. "Jeff got a football scholarship to the University of Georgia and had a short acting career in NYC before he became an attorney." Perhaps his more limited **depth of feeling** (light line writer) and **short residual memory** of his sensory and life emotional experiences, limited his ability to communicate deep emotions and strong opinions to an audience that we most often see in very successful actors. Jeff went on to become a successful lawyer bringing together the combination of traits above and his capacity to roam freely in intellectual ethical matters and relate well to others. He probably kept track of most all of his classmates at every school he has ever attended. So I'm telling you this, he's the one I'll call shortly to get some good stories about all of our classmates, location and occupation.

---

[7]   Metzler, Mary MGA (Master Grapho Analyst) in <u>Letters of the Alphabet,</u> 1981.

SUBJECT 9D

1363 W. Nancy Creek C
N.E. Atlanta Ga.
April, 21, 1966

Dear Major Batchelder
We enjoyed the field trip very
much, I liked the simulator best,
Boy that was neat!! I never
thought airplanes were so big
until we came to the Base,
Everything was very interesting.
Love,
Malinda, Stary
L

(#4)

SUBJECT 9D
HOMEBODY - (Malinda S.)

Malinda is a "**cool-headed**" young girl (most of her "upstrokes" are a near vertical slant to slightly left of vertical). She also exhibits persistent, though not strong, **withdrawal from others**; her **self-interest** (vertical writing) meant that she made decisions that suited her best. Further, that she distanced herself from her past and others, and the future is seen in the wide left and right margins, respectively. Her relatively short "t's" and "d's" stems gave us further proof that she was unlikely to seek help from others due to her **independence** trait. Most of her classmates didn't feel judged by her since she did not generally **express her feelings** about them (vertical slanted upstrokes). This is a trait that many leaders possess; their subordinates don't feel judged. Again, she was **holding on to the past** and **family security**. She will do things to attract others to her as she has a strong **desire for attention** (final strokes that curve up and back over ending letter).

1308 Brooklawn
Atlanta, Georgia
April 21, 1966

Dear Major Batchelder,

Thank you so much for inviting us to see Doberins. We had so much fun! It was very interesting, especially the simulator! I never knew there was anything like that!

It was a lot of fun going up into the tower and even in the airplane! I'd never been to an air force Base in my life and I surely enjoyed it! Thanks again.

Sincerely,
Cindy Lovett

SUBJECT 9E
TOUGH ON SELF - (Cindy L)

April 1966, Cindy lived primarily **in-the-present** (proportionately limited extension of the up and down strokes from the baseline); these strokes (in the middle zone) also meant that she had **less desire for change** or new horizons. Note also t-bars are "on-the-deck" or "below-the-deck" (i.e., below the top of the case letters). These very low t-bars indicated very **low self-esteem**. At that time, she had very few goals. Combining Cindy's above-mentioned traits and her **security needs** (very narrow left margin) I knew that she wouldn't venture far from home.

1326 Old Johnson's Fy.
Atlanta, Georgia

Dear Major Batchelder,

Thank you for inviting me to the Dobbins air force base. It was fun going through all those planes. I especially liked going in that simulator, mat, plane. I was the pilot and my friend Steve Allen was the navigator. I went through a storm with lightning.

Another thing I want to thank you for was just the pleasure of getting out of school and much work.

Sincerely yours,
Paul West

SUBJECT 9F
HONESTY - (Paul W.)

Honesty stands out when there is no "looping", or "retracing" especially in a's and o's. Paul had especially fine **precision** and **manual dexterity/engineering** or **artistic** aptitude (squared "r's"); he chose a few friends carefully (note the thin "y" loops). He had an excellent sense of **rhythm** (even spacing between his letters and words); this rhythm trait helped him accomplish more work. His **nurturing** talent was seen in the cupping of his capital "I's" (at the base of the "I's"). The generally right slanted upstrokes (over 50 degrees) meant that he could **empathize** with others and **express his feelings**. Most all of his traits then, suited him to be a teacher or medical professional. His friends and family had to appreciate his **generosity** (frequent broad final upstrokes in his words and no squeezing of the spacing between his letters).

4343 Ashwoody Tr.
Atlanta Ga. 30319
April 21, 1966

Dear Major Batchelder,
Thank you for arranging the field trip for us. It was very exciting. I liked the simulator and the tower but I thought the weather room and the plane were the best parts of the field trip. Thanks again,

Sincerely,
Steve Moddelmog

SUBJECT 9G
VENTURING OUT - (Steve M.)

Venturing out is evident in the wide margins left and right side of Steve's letter meant that he was not as **dependent** on his past or family (need for security). **Poise** was seen in his dealings with others (25 degrees ± right slanted upstrokes). Mentally he preferred to be **physically active** rather than a spectator (loops in his "p's"). His many fine traits included **honesty** (clear, not retraced left side of his "a" and "o's"), and **broad-mindedness** (broad shaped "o's" and "a's"). His healthy **self-esteem** showed in his practical intermediate range goals (t-bars above the case letters and on-the-stems).* Steve had good relationships with both his father and his mother (balanced lower and vertical loop in capital "I"). Steve had all the traits of a **leader** who has his act together. His relationships are well managed. He had the aptitude and skills to excel in many fields and he seemed to be free of personality defects.

---

*T-bars consistently off-the-stem indicates a person's thinking or activity may be in-the-clouds and very unrealistic. However if the t-bar is not far off-the-stem but is combined with a heavy down pressure (**will power**), the subject may, if his other enhancing traits are present, still land his lofty goals.

3878 Raine Ct.
April. 21. 1966
Atlanta, Ga.

Dear Major Batchelder

Thank you for taking us on a tour of Dobbins Air Force Base. I had alot of fun seeing the raft, airplane, simulator and the tower and many things. I liked seeing the way you went to Viet Nam. I learned about the two men over England and they thought that they were going some place and in about ½ an hour one man looked out the window and said that looks just like the place we

SUBJECT 9H
GOOD MEMORY - (Larry B.)

If all of your i's are dotted close to the stem and your t's are crossed, then you've got a **memory** like Larry. Narrow left margins meant that he had a **need for security** satisfied through involvement with family and others.   Also his narrow left margin indicated **thriftiness** and **desire for popularity**. Family is important to him; and you can see that his capital "I's" have balanced loops (vertical loop "mother" and horizontal "father").   A very narrow right margin indicated he's was likely a good "mixer" and **not inhibited**. Further enhancing his social skills, was his 45-degree plus rightward slanted upstrokes; this meant that he had an inclination to **empathize** with others and **express** his own **feelings**. He was good at **analyzing** situations and problems by digging into facts (sawtooth "m's" and "n's"). "V" shaped "m's" and "n's" mean **analytical thinking** and inverted "v" shapes means **exploratory thinking**. His strong **determination** was found in his straight "y" downstrokes. Another trait that enhanced his problem solving was his good **memory** (i.e., dotting "i's" and crossing "t's"). His learning ability was further helped by his **cumulative thinking** (i.e., his block writing meant that he attached facts to a structure or pattern).   In his letter* he demonstrated his exceptional thinking patterns when he recalled a WWII aircraft caught in a jet stream headwind unable to make progress over a point on the ground. This showed Larry's good memory about an unusual phenomena (the headwind speed equaled the aircraft's air speed)**.

were over a half an hour ago.

Sincerely

Larry B

*Similar to Don W's **Parking Lot Rage** where personality strokes/traits matched his **anger**, **sarcasm** and **paranoia**, we have another example of the writer's messages fitting perfectly with their personality strokes/traits.

**Years ago a similar situation occurred over a Greenland ice cap where a bomber going about 180 miles per hour actually made a landing on a high ice plateau; because of the headwind their ground speed was near zero at touch down. When the crew looked out the window they realized they were no longer airborne.

1309 Rustic Ridge
Atlanta, Ga.
April 21, 1966

Dear Major Batchelder,

I want to thank you for inviting and taking us to the Airforce Base. It was one of the nicest trips I have ever taken. Best of all I liked the simulator. It was really like being in one. I just wanted you to know I appreciated it.

Sincerely,
Debbie
Morgan

SUBJECT 9I
EMOTIONALLY WITHDRAWN - (Debbie M.)

In April 21st, 1966, she is a leftward-slanted upstrokes writer **emotionally withdrawn**. Was she a left handed or right handed person?* I inquired January 20, 2003 and she's right handed!** As for Debbie's prominent traits: **manual dexterity** (squared "r's") **organizational skill** (balanced f-loops); **attention to details** (dotting "i's" and crossing "t's"); **a sense of humor** (curving, bent initial strokes on her capital letters): (see "Rustic Ridge", "Major", and "Batchelder" et. al.). Her thinking pattern is **cumulative** (block type letter formation). Cumulative thinking means that she initiates her thinking by having a pattern or structure to which she can attach her facts. She had good relationships with her father and mother (both loops in capital "I's" are balanced). Notice how she has succeeded well in **conforming** to the guidelines for the heights of her letter strokes.

Excellent rhythm showed in her even spacing between letters and words. The final letters in her words rising up and back toward herself meant she worked at **drawing attention to herself**. **Independence** in her work (short t-stems) and personal life (d-stems short) was evident. Her heavier down pressure strokes showed **depth of feelings**. With all of her above talents and desire to draw attention to herself, she had the aptitude to become an actress.

---

*I believe it's generally accepted by most handwriting analysts that the slant of the upstrokes in writing has the same meaning whether or not a person is left handed or right handed.

**Many left-handed and leftward slant writers tell me how difficult it is to write from left to right. The rules, with broad consensus among professionals, say that you can't look at handwriting and determine that a person is left or right handed; nor can you determine age or sex, though common traits may statistically appear more often in the same sex or age groups.

4064 Chippewa Pl, NE
Atlanta 19, Georgia 30319
April 21, 1966

Dear Major Batchelder,

I really thank you for taking us on the feild trip Tuesday. I liked touring the M. A. T. airplane because I have never been up close to a real toransport plane before. I still wish I could have a simulater in my room.

Sincerly,
David Williams

SUBJECT 9J
HESITANCY - (David W.)

David W. presents an unusual pattern of an exaggerated amount of spacing between his words. Before proceeding, it's as though he is reflecting on his next words and his past words. This accented further his **hesitation** and repeated **procrastination** traits (t-bars not completing beyond the stem). **Quick understanding** in his thinking shows in the needlepoints in his "r's". Pay attention to his **manual dexterity** and **artistic talents** (squared "r's"); these strokes are also seen in engineers. Frequent application of his **determination** trait is found in his straight "y" downstrokes. **Analytical** thinking in "v's", shaped "n's" and "m's", plus **exploratory** (thinking inverted or saw toothed angular shaped "m's" and "n's"). The connection with mother shows in the capital I-looped upstroke, while a very limited involvement with his father at this point in time (horizontal capital I-loop). For the "rest of the story" I'll have to locate David now 37 years later!

4384 Cander Lake
Circle.
Atlanta, Ga.
April 21, 1966

Dear Major Batchelder,
    Thank-you for arranging
and taking us on a tour of
Dobbins Air Force Base. I
especially enjoyed the simulator
and the tower. It was very
interesting and lots of fun.
I do not think I have
gone on such a nice field
trip.

                    Sincerly,
                    Jane Setterstrom

SUBJECT 9K
SUPPRESSION & WORRY - (Jane S.)

By now most of you readers should be jumping ahead of me and telling me what you saw in Jane's strokes. I saw much **procrastination** (incomplete t-bars), **open-minded** (wide-eyed "e's"). She is capable of being a young **worry** wart (loops within her "m's" and "n's"). Cramping in the final strokes and "m's" and "n's" and in some cases in her "r's" showed that she had **emotional restriction** of expression (or artistic talent) and there is much more that I could talk about here but this is not the time or place for discussion of any psychological restrictions of this 11-year-old. If I could have met her parents and teachers 37 years ago, I would have pointed to Jane's worry and procrastination and perhaps this might have accelerated the efforts to work on her aptitudes and skills and overcome her worries and procrastination. For the rest of the story 2003, we would have to talk with Jane and find out how she dealt with her youth concerns.

Dear Major Batchelder,

Thank you so very much for arranging a wonderful field trip for our class. The two parts I liked best were going up in the tower and going in the simulator. I have never flown in my life before, but I hope to be able to fly soon. I had a wonderful time. I am sure everyone else did too

and I hope I can come back soon.

Sincerly,

Lee Anne

SUBJECT 9L
AN ARTIST? – (Lee Anne)

Immediately I saw a young lady with **deep feelings** (heavier down pressure in her writing compared with most all of her classmates). This means she accumulated all of the **sensory** information (sight, sounds, touch, smell, experiences); their richness whether positive or negative remained with her making her "every moment of the day meaningful." Unusually good **color sense** (in clear, heavy lines), **precision, organization** (balanced f-loops) and **manual dexterity** (squared "r's"), she had the traits that combined for great aptitude for **expression in art** (paintings?). What could have held Lee Anne back at this point in life? She had **low expectations** for herself (no goals beyond here and now, t-bars below low). She **can take critique** and suggestions for dealing with her restrictions as no loops in her "t's" and "d's" show (i.e., she is not **sensitive to criticism**)*. She had the **desire mentally** to be in the action **physically** (remember that large loops depending on where they occur enhance our capacity to absorb more information, people, ideas and thoughts). Notice now her "fat" p-loops, and if you review her letter at age 11 she was already hoping "to be able to fly soon", further proof of her desire to be **physically active**. Lee Ann is inclined to loop a lot (i.e., she tells "stories"; see left side strokes that loop in a's and o's). Summarizing the primary traits, Lee Ann employs for any artistic efforts, I see her deep feelings, fine color sense, precision, manual dexterity, and organization.

Very rounded letters are indicative of Lee Ann's **loving** nature; that she could become a great teacher or in the healing profession is seen in her cupped capital "I's". This is an illustration of how a teacher using handwriting analysis could encourage her students to set goals and move on to achieve.

*She is open-minded and broad-minded enough to try change; note the wide "e's" "o's",and "a's", respectively.

SUBJECT 914

4001 Navajo Trail
Atlanta 19, Georgia
April 2, 1966

Dear Major Batchelder,

Thank you for arranging the tour of Dobbin's Air Force Base. It was very interesting to see all the different instruments and seeing or knowing a little of them is very interesting, too. The simulator was both interesting and fun. I don't think I'll ever forget it.

Sincerely,
Hack Heyward

SUBJECT 9M
THE VOLUNTEER - (Hack H.)

The first thing I noticed in Hack's writing was the circle beginning his capital letters in "Navajo", "Major", and "Force" (**desire for responsibility***); he would be the one who volunteered to chair or serve a group. Second, I noticed his persistent **self-consciousness** (remember the final humps in "m's" and "n's" being above the previous; those letters appeared often with a high degree of trait intensity). He was a very **thoughtful** person; notice the unusual length between his words indicating **hesitation**. He had excellent **rhythm** (even spacing between his letters and words). His best friend from '66 informed me (1/19/03) that he is a very successful president of a corporation in Oregon. At the time of his writing (4/66) he had no long or short range **goals** in mind (very low t-bars) and had low **self-esteem**. Obviously, things changed in his life and his handwriting strokes would have changed later to show the shift in his personality as he lifted his goals and marched on to success.

---

*A small initial stroke winding back indicates **jealousy** trait; but when a much larger loop back is present, then a person has a desire to assume responsibility in his activities with others.

SUBJECT 9N

1365 Brooklawn Rd. N.E. 30319

Atlanta, Ga.

april 21, 1966

Dear Major Batchelder,

My name is Danny Machado and I want to thank you and all of the men who took us to all the places on the Base. when I grow up I wanted to go join the navy at first but then I asked the my father which he would would join and he said the air force I liked the air force all the time. Thank Lt. Williams for all the fun and I thank you for the whole time there and for taking just for us. and I might go there again and talk to you and Lt. Williams. it might not be fun but I would like to see you and Lt. Williams

SUBJECT 9N
PROCRASTINATION - (Danny M.)

In spite of the lined school paper providing benchmarks of minimum height for letters, Danny has the smallest size writing of any of his classmates. This indicates his trait of **concentration**; a 'global' trait that will intensify all of his other traits. The second trait I spotted was his **perfectionism** (shown with words or spelling crossed out or changed).

Irritability showed in the flicks, jabs, or short dashes of his i-dots; and his **impatience** to get on with the future is seen in instances where his i-dots are far right of his stems. Note here in the message he wrote about wanting to "join the Navy when I grow up". However he talked with his father and said that he decided that he "liked the Air Force after all." Confirming further that this 11-year-old was thinking about **goals** further out in time than most of his classmates, notice that he had many of his t-bars high but still on the stems (practical) goals. Danny's balanced f-loops showed that he was well **organized**.

Procrastination often got in the way of his actions (t-bars stopping at the stems). The connections with his father and mother look healthy (capital I-loops balanced); and again his letter verifies this as he asks for his dad's advice about which service was best to join. A comprehensive analysis would have helped sort out the various areas or aspects of his developing personality. As Danny overcomes his weaknesses, leading with his ability to **concentrate** his thinking and his **decisiveness** (short abrupt final strokes), I would not be surprised to learn that he became a high achiever.* Incidentally, Danny had the smallest writing of all 42 classmates. My next book will cover this and the outcomes of his classmates.

---

*Wide left margin tells me that Danny is **not dependent** as many are on the security concerns of many young people, and has a good relationship with parents, likely acceptance.

SUBJECT 90

1181 Lake Hearn
Atlanta, Georgia 30
April 21, 1966

Dear Major Batchelder,
    We all enjoyed our visit to Dobbi
Air Force Base. That is the biggest ba
I have ever seen. Everybody has been
talking about it ever since tuesday
evening. I enjoyed the simulator very
much. It felt like it was really mov
g. Most of all I enjoyed the airplane a
the tower. I got to see a green plan
come in for a touchdown. We sure
did enjoy it, thanks again.
                        Sincerely,
                        Randy Bone

SUBJECT 9O
A LOYAL LEADER - (Randy B.)

Randy was a leader among the "coolest" of heads in his class. Having consistently near vertical upstrokes demonstrated his **poise** and **ability to make decisions** based more on his head than his heart. Since he doesn't exhibit the far right slanted upstrokes of those who are more inclined to express their feelings, his associates don't feel judged by him (though he will still have his opinions, they are not often **expressed**). This trait is often seen in leaders. Other traits supporting his leadership skills, include **loyalty** (round i-dots), **organization** (balanced f-loops), **determination** (straight downstrokes of his "y's" and "j's"), **pride** in his d-stems (2½ times height case letters) and t-stems; his **goals** are all **practical** (on his t-stems) and the rhythm (spacing even) excellent. The absence of left and right margins suggested that he would have been very **frugal**, and that he had a **need to communicate** with others, and that he could have been strongly focused on money. This combination of all the above traits with his **pride** (high "t" or d-stems) would have propelled him to succeed beyond his financial needs.

3968 Ashford Dunwoody Road
April 21, 1966
Atlanta, Georgia

Dear Major Batchelder,
    Our whole class enjoyed the tour through Dobbins Air Force Base. Even though we're going to the C.D.C. today Mrs. Wells & Mrs. Bullen both agree that it won't be as exciting as the trip on Tuesday.
    In case you don't remember me I was in your group and am glad I was (even though most of group was boys).
    The three things I liked best was the airplane, the simulator and the tower (even though I didn't go all the way up).
    I think all the people at Dobbins

SUBJECT 9P
A POISED POLITICIAN - (Jackie C.)

I've just finished talking about a leader* type personality and now here we are observing Jackie. She is a young lady who looks quite compatible** with Randy B (Subject 9O) because her upstrokes are near vertical like his (though often more to the right). Looking at the strokes that support her leadership ability, I find that she has **practical goals** and **excellent rhythm** (even spacing words and letters), **broad-minded** (broad "a's" and "o's"); **gregariousness** (larger sized writing than her classmate Randy B), indicating she felt more **self-important** (larger capital letters). At this point in time Jackie had some signs of **jealousy** (small initial loops to left seen in words "Major, "Ms.", "Wells", "Force", and "Tuesday"). Looking at the capital "I's" I see that the relationship with her father was more limited than with her mother (loop vertical). Would this explain that Jackie might have been vying for attention with a sibling? Loops in her "p's" show that she would enjoy active **physical** participation in the world of sports. Her **precision** and **rhythm** meant that she had a good **sense of timing** and her block writing indicated that she would prefer playing with an overall game plan in mind.

Looking at Jackie's combination of traits, I can easily see her as playing political games in her work or social circles and assuming a leadership role.

---

*Generally it is estimated that about 15%± of population writes near vertical slant of upstrokes.

**The major compatibility points of two or more persons (personal or business association), will be seen by the like slanting of the upstrokes and similar depth of the down pressure of their writing instruments. This along with other global traits (slant weight loops, size of writing and rhythm) will give us the indications for compatibility. Differences in personality traits can make for interesting and exciting experiences. But likeness in traits makes for comfort and understanding.

SUBJECT 10
CAUTION, CAREFUL... (Ruth Rigid)

Ruth is on the fence, betwixt using her head or her heart to make decisions (upstrokes fall equally between being **reserved**, under 45 degree right slant; and over 45 degree slant where there is more inclination to express **emotion**, barring other traits which restrict impulses).

Ruth's struggle is the inclination to express **feelings** and **impulses** (far right slanting strokes); further compounded by **liberal tendencies** (wide separation between letters), and **generosity** (broad final upstrokes of last letters). Extraordinary efforts to control her thinking and actions is evident in the **rigidity** of her strokes that lack **imagination** (no loops in letters); **caution** is in the straight strokes between letters; **steadiness** in the very straight baselines, and her intense efforts at **perfection** (controlled left margin). A profession that requires **caution** and yet **quick comprehension** (needle points on "r's") and **precision** (even lines and formation of letters) and good **rhythm** (even spacing between letters and words) are all combined in one package in Ruth. The medical field records maintenance fits perfectly.

Blacksmith and Wagonmaker.

REPAIRING DONE PROMPTLY.

Aprile 9th 1887

Mr Judy
friend Sir will
it be all wright for
Me to make Miss
Mc   a wagon on the
Claim she has against
The Estate of
Dec. if so please advise
Me at once i will make her
One Which she wants
Very bad
I am yours Duly

SUBJECT 11
REAL OR COUNTERFEIT? - Jacob's World

A late 19th Century blacksmith and wagonmaker from a Civil War "border" state, Jacob had great empathy for others (far forward slant of upstrokes). He received a Presidential Pardon after serving fourteen months of his sentence because he was greatly admired for his skills and demeanor by his warden and politicians alike.

Emotionally, he was highly "inclined" to **respond** to others (see the measured far forward slant of his stokes). However I'll soon tell you about his other social traits that limited his connection with others. Jacob harbored **deep** and **lasting** feelings from all his sensory and human experiences (though our photocopy is limiting, I judged his stroke down pressure to be moderate to heavy).

While he was mentally inclined to **dominate** others (see downward slant of t-crossbars), it wasn't heavy (crossbars lighter down pressure). His **diplomatic** trait made it likely that his manner was soft spoken, which tempered his dominating nature (see the receding size of his letters especially in his "my's" that show diplomacy, especially when he referred to his lady friend, Miss "M", and to himself in "me"). Interceding for Miss "M" writing about her claim in his letter to the judge, he showed his **temper**, possible irritation with the legal system, when he formed the "t" crossbar in "wants" (this cross stroke t-bar began after the stem - see footnote[8]). Yet, when we see the words he chose in his letter we don't see his temper. His strong intuition is seen in the repeated instances of breaks between his letters. Therefore, I assume he was excellent at reading others.

Jacob protected himself from becoming too close to others by being very selective in his choice of friends (note the thin loop in the "g" in "wright", 4th line; again seen in the "y" in "yours truly").

Was Jacob escaping from his past family and business set backs? The margins left side of his letter (convex), along with weak upstroke pen pressures indicate **hesitant** venturing out. It also shows reflection on returning to his past known

---

[8]   We are subject to our emotional conditions, of the moment, as stroke and letter formations are different than we are taught due to the impact of our emotions. An example is the difficulty an angry boxer has in landing his punches with precision.

"safety points" versus the future unknown, people and places; see his very wide right side margins, from which he was attempting to distance himself. Another trait stroke pointing to the **isolation** Jacob felt at this point in time from both his past, his family, his future and others (1887) is evident in the tiny capital "I" letter (9th line). This very small size "I" is associated with feelings of **inadequacy**. Once again all of these traits combined led to his choice of a criminal sideline because when people are in the process of doing something illegal or immoral they often hide from family and others. Confirming this likelihood are the return strokes of his "y's" which turn away from his sensual "fulfillment". About this time he was three years from separating from his first wife. If he was receiving fulfillment in his relationship these wide return strokes would have come up to the baseline. Incidentally, only three of his eight children, that he had with his first wife, survived to 1900. Imagine his hurt.

I looked at his aptitudes; the traits he used in his primary trade as blacksmith/wagonmaker. I noticed the **precision** in his letter formations and attention to details (dotting "i's" and crossing "t's"). His excellent **color sense** is indicated in his heavy and clear writing lines. Strong **analytical** and **exploratory** mental traits contribute to his considerable mental prowess (the sawtooth "m's" and "n's").

We all know that about the time of his writing (age 27) his money situation was affected by the railroad boom and bust. He likely had difficulty supporting his family and suffered the multiple deaths of his children. During this period, his father after a long illness as a result of service in the Civil War had just died. He then had the responsibility for his mother and three young siblings in addition to his own family. Remember, his writing slants shows his inclination to empathize with others; in other words, he is touched by what happens to others. Remember he was isolating himself from his past, family and others at this time. Did he harbor anger against the federal government? (He was from a border state and lived in the aftermath of the Civil War). Were these contributing factors in his decision to make counterfeit money? Remember the Presidential Pardon we referred to earlier? Jacob had great diplomatic skills and I judged him to be soft spoken - a "charmer". Oh yes! The rest of the story after prison: He proceeded to persuade a financially well-off lady in another state from a prominent family to marry him. He went on to experience a very successful business career and have five more children who lived good long lives.

Miss Betty Ann Jaggers.
Dormitory III Room 305
A.P.I.
Auburn,
Ala

Wednesday

My Darling Daughter
      Your letter came to me here at the
office yesterday and it did me so much
good to again be assured that mother and
I have been so successfull in raising
daughters who understand that whatever
we do or what decision we make it
is always done with the thought that
it is best for your wellfare and future
happiness.
      It hurts both of us very much to
make decisions where we feel that it is
against your feeling of proper consideration.
We try never to make a selfish decision
and although we are not always with
you and Dorothy there is one worry we

We are expecting to go down to Uncle Clem's Sunday to try to help them out with something about the Church at Crawfordville. Mother and I went to the Football game last Saturday and really saw a good one. We have tickets to the Tech-Alabama game Saturday but the Bondurant's can't come over.

Hope you have plenty of water to keep clean.

We will be looking forward to your coming home for Thanksgiving and again tell you I appreciate your letter and you are certainly forgiven for everything you did or said in haste.

Love,
Daddy

SUBJECT 12
PERMISSION NOT GRANTED!
- (MARSHALL OLIVER)

Setting: Atlanta, Georgia.
Time: Fall of '54
Characters: Marshall Oliver Saggus, proud and prominent architect and father.
                 Betty Ann, Marshall Oliver's pretty, vivacious, impulsive and strong-willed daughter.
Situation: Permission to attend an off-campus football weekend - denied.
Scene One: Betty Ann has returned to her Auburn campus dormitory. She regrets her departing home outburst over her father's decision. She writes a letter of apology. Marshall Oliver's letter response and envelope address gives us an excellent example as to how our emotions can intensify our written strokes/traits. Notice on the envelope Marshall Oliver's downward slanted t-bars crossbar in "Betty" (**dominance**). This trait of exercising control over others is far more pronounced than his slightly downward t-bars. When he was reflecting on her letter, the greater than usual downward t-bars shows up again in the word "yesterday". Pointing to other strong traits seen in Marshall Oliver's letter will help us to picture his personality. Though I've never met him, with handwriting analysis I'm able to see in his letter his many outstanding traits that include: Very strong **pride** (tall "t" and d-stems) and great **determination** (long downstrokes in his "y's"), very **impulsive** behavior (over 60 degrees right slanting upstrokes); this also is a trait that tells us that he has great feeling or **empathy** for others. Being overly **sensitive to criticism** about himself is indicated in the several instances of the very fat d-loops (he blew out of proportion any criticism he received wherever you saw fat loops in his letter). Though his **self-consciousness** was not excessive, it still is present in his "m" and "n's" where the final humps are above the previous. This trait combines with his sensitivity to criticism and his empathy for others to explain the lengths he goes to play his "tough love" father's role. While he gives his disciplinary rules, it still hurts him to do so.

Betty Ann recalls that after a football game in Atlanta, she sought his permission to go to a dance club with a group. Her father informed her that this club had recently been raided. Betty Ann said, "But I'm 21!" to which Marshall Oliver replied, you go right ahead but, please remember you're a **Saggus**. Just be sure that if the club is raided again tonight your picture will not appear in our morning paper." She chose not to go.

Note: 1954 college dorm rules at Auburn University where boy/girl ratio was 7.5:1: Parental permission was required for a return to campus dorm after curfew, or for overnight stays off campus.

Kristin B

Dec 23 1942

Indianapolis, Indiana

~~Now~~ is the time for ~~all~~ good people to
use Talcon steel special design t save
costs with less steel!

I am a lefty!

SUBJECT 13 a
" 13 b

13a

Terry O'B

April 13, 1942

Cleveland Ohio

Write now is the time for
all good people to use Talcon
Steel special design to save
costs with less steel.

Jeff Landed

#13b

SUBJECTS 13A&B
I'M A LEFTY – (Kristine and Terrence)

Kristine is emotionally **withdrawn** nearly half the time (upstrokes left of vertical); she is very **composed** the other half of the time (near vertical and right slanted under 30 degrees). Her **depth-of-emotion** is generally light (a light pressure with pen); this means that memories of her experiences will fade faster.

She has many fine qualities, including good **precision** (formation of letters), plus the mental desire to be **physically active** (loops in p's), very **broad-minded** (broad a's and o's), excellent **rhythm** (spacing words and letters are even), and strong **pride** (height of t-stems) in her work.

Kristine's "ace" is her **intuition** (gaps between letters after the first two). While she's **venturing-out** (increasing left margin) she has much **hesitancy** or fear of the future (very wide right margin). **Creativity** is seen in her printed letters mixed with cursive. With very **practical goals** (t-bars on stems) and being quite **direct** (no upstrokes on t's) she has the aptitude to succeed.

For contrast, I've added another "lefty", Terrance O'B, who has very far forward slanted upstrokes (over 65 degrees) close to all the time. This generally indicates, assuming no reductive traits, a very **impulsive**, **expressive** person who has an **opinion** on most everything. He has an inclination to **physically** get into most activities (the loops in his p's). Terence and Kristine should give you further evidence that people will express their mental and emotional qualities in their writing strokes without regard to whether they are left or right handed.

Looking at compatibility of the above two characters, likenesses in slants of upstrokes are associated with compatibility. A second major determinant of compatibility is the same downward pressure using the writing instrument. So two individuals, one with very left slanted upstrokes (**withdrawn**) versus the other with very far right upstrokes, (**expressive/impulsive**) will have difficulty empathizing with each other. A second major determinant of compatibility is the downward pressure of the writing instrument. The same downward pressure generally means that two people will grow at about the same rate, if they have the same writing pressure depth. In other words, they will be ready to move from one new experience to another at about the same rate. However, common values and culture is the glue that can hold two people together in spite of handwriting stroke/trait differences; because this commonality removes much of the material for arguments (i.e., how their values concerning money and relationships match).

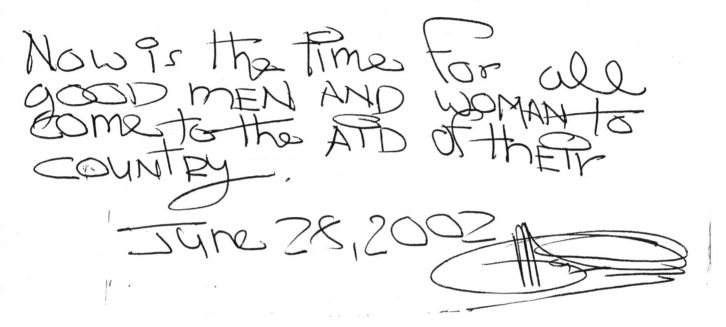

SUBJECT 14
DAVID IS GOLIATH – (David T)

Salesman David T is one-of-a- kind; a very **creative**, **artistic** talent that wows all around him. Stopping all others is his physically imposing 6 foot 7 inch, 265 pound frame. His intense heavy strokes* alerted me to his **deep emotional** makeup; and this **depth** also meant that he would retain the memory of all of his life's sensual impressions (sight, sound, touch, smell, taste). Every moment of the day he lives to the fullest. Those clear heavy lines tell us that he has a rich **sense of color** and **line appreciation**** that are present in gifted artists. His writing reminded me of Walt Disney's writing and signature.

Creativity shows in his presentations (mixing of cursive and printed letters). You can't miss the large circled i-dots for they are a sign of his **desire** to be **unique**; and their size suggests some child-like behavior. Is he a cut-up or **whimsical** character in public? I know that he has to be very much into everything, every moment of the day because his strokes are intense*** **living in the present**

(everyday world) can be expected from those whose strokes are confined to the "middle zone"; that is they aren't venturing into the **philosophical**, **theoretical** realms of those whose strokes reach well into the "upper zone". So, David's unique **emotional** and **mental** makeup allows him to summon all of his colorful life experiences and creatively captivate his audiences. The stylistic flourishes of his signature communicates the persona of a **showman**. Though his very large stature commands attention, he could still stage shows that would amaze the decision makers of the large corporations that bought his computer systems.

Most others may think they know David because his manner conveys the idea that he relates well to all; but, his near vertical strokes (75%) tell me a different story. He doesn't usually **express** his true **feelings** to others. He leads with his head to do what fits him best rather than be influenced by someone else who pulls at his heartstrings. Because he does not usually express his feelings; they will accumulate and remain for long periods of time (heavy down pressure of strokes); then when some precipitating event occurs, his dam bursts with all the accumulated emotions and experiences. You will have a scene full of sound and fury!

While David is mostly **upbeat** (up slanted T-bars), his **pessimism** (gentle downward trend of his lines) tempers his becoming too **enthusiastic** (longer t-bars). With so many interacting strokes between his lines, I knew he had many irons-in-the-fire that would assure the success he told me about when he applied all of his exceptional talents.

*His pen's markings could be seen all the way through to the 5th page of the pad he wrote on.

**People like David with clear heavy writing strokes get more out of life and live with the richness of life and past experiences with memories that last.

***He's a frequent scuba diver fully equipped, camera and all, excited by the panoramic views of the ocean floors.

SUBJECT 15
JOHNNIE B GOOD – (Johnnie B)

Sharp as a tack with his quick comprehension (high needle points on r's and in s's and some n's), Johnnie has many traits combining to account for his making his way well in life: His goals are first about all **practical** (t-bars on stems). **Optimistic** (steady uptrend of baselines). **Excellent rhythm** (spacing letters and words); I'd bet the ladies have found him to be a good dancer. His **warmth** will be easily felt in his **expression of feelings** (70 degrees far right slanted upstrokes). **Precision** in shaping his strokes. Continuous **enthusiasm** seen in his long t-bars. He can defend himself well with **sarcasm** (fade-out t-bar barbs). Don't try to take over his work because he will show his **independence** (very short t-stems).

The finer things in life are important to him, too; look at the Greek e's indicative of **literary** appreciation; and, he is both **analytical** (v's in m's and n's and h's) and **exploratory** in his thinking (sawtooth inverted v's, m's, n's, and h's). Is he a writer? I must interview him!

Now is the time for all good men to come to the aid of their country.

Johnnie B.

Steve Solomon — Comedian

It was a pleasure meeting you

thanks

S. Solomon

Two whores walked into a bar ...

STANDUP COMIC   SUBJECT 169th

Now is the time for all
good men and women
to come to the aid of
their country!

Peter Sasso

SUBJECT 16
STAND-UP FOR COMICS – (Steve and Peter)

Steve possesses the attributes to delight his audiences. He can **empathize** with others (over 75% of his upstrokes are slanted over 60 degrees right) and his **intuition** (breaks between his letters) allows him to sense his audience and quickly relate with snappy remarks. Being **physically active** (p-loops) his body language can supplement his words. Most good entertainers are **opinionated** on many matters, which makes them far more interesting than neutral, objective personalities. (Far right slanted strokes are present in impulsive opinionated people).

Like Steve, Peter has the fundamental traits to support his trade. The sharp-pointed opinions (shown in his far right slanted upstrokes). Next, the experiences in his past, including the memory of his accumulated hurts (deep **resentments** seen in his stiff, below-the-baseline initial upstrokes) provide great material for his **humor, good sense of rhythm** (showed in even spacings). Think about how his good rhythm helped his timing of jokes. Peter has an **independent** streak in his work (very short t-stems in 'the'). Peter will bring more philosophical ideas into his humor (greater relative height of his upstrokes into upper zone) than Steve.

STEADY AS SHE GOES – (Captain Hoydal)

Responsible for over two thousand passengers and crew sailing the seven seas Captain Hoydal has all the "right stuff" you'd want to see. His own **even keel (stable and steady** is seen in baseline) with a **sense of timing (rhythm** in even spacing) to lead and sense all the necessary departments serving those onboard while sensing how to safely maneuver his mammoth ship's movements through narrow straits, storms and tides.

Engineering talent is evident in his squared r's with **creativity** in printed letters mixed with cursive. **Precision** in his letters formation. **Optimism** found in his up-slanted baselines. **Attention-to-details** (dot i's and crossing t's). **Empathy** with his passengers and crews; he demonstrated this in his public appearances and warm introductions of his staff at the captain's reception. Medium down pressure of writing means that he will retain emotional and sensory experiences with **depth**, but not for extended duration.

Generally **conservative** (letters are close to each other) and not given to flights of fancy (i.e. limited **imagination** and no t-bars off the stems) he will pay attention to the tasks at hand. Note that in his signature, his message to the public, he projects more **imagination** (loops into the philosophical/theoretical planes) than he really employs. His **energy** and **will power** (t-bars) are short lived, meaning he will rely more on **intuition**, **planning** and **rhythm** to perform his duties of providing safe and entertaining cruises.

Now is the time for all good men and woman to come to the aid of their country

John Hoydal.

Josh —

The suggestion for discussion
was good — and for today.

Perhaps we should talk when
you come back from lunch —
Before removing the other items —

That will free up my afternoon —
I'll be back here — soon —

J

SUBJECT 18
MS. NASTY NICE – (J.S.)

This subject's hurried note is about a "touchy" situation; and, it's an excellent specimen to illustrate how our emotions of the moment can shift, for some more easily than others. Also, a good example is presented where a case of negative strokes/traits combined to form a short lived "perfect storm": And for good reason the practical desired outcome for the writer resulted in a shift to more positive strokes in the second half of the note.

You've heard it said that a person was so mad they couldn't "see straight". In J.S's note early-on her t-bars repeatedly began after the stem (**temper**). Also, it's well understood and I'm sure experienced by most that anger can make one **stiff** or shaky (see the uneven up and down strokes lines).

Now let's look at her other strokes/traits that combined to form J.S.'s short **emotional outburst***: Her variable upstroke slants (mostly far rightward) showed her expressing her **feelings** (with temper) then pulling back toward the vertical slant at times. The more objective 'cool headed' head-over-heart). Early **pessimism** in the note (downward slanted baselines); then shifting later to an upward **optimistic** approach (slanted up baselines). Also, her t-bars (the last two) slanted upward (**upbeat**); knowing the situation, I suspect she was hopeful of gaining a more favorable result. **Caution** (the straight stroke lines at the end of each line) appeared in the last part of her note. So what 'global' trait contributed to her ability to overcome her initial pessimism, temper and tightness? It was her very light line writing (**depth of feelings**, emotions that can fade fast); other more subtle strokes/traits were present that enhanced or modified her resultant behavior; but this brief description of prominent traits, objective versus a comprehensive analysis, is to highlight major points and avoid obscuring central themes with too much detail. With Ms. "Nasty Nice" specimen I'm illustrating a writer's strokes negative emotion, not clear in her written message; then I've pointed to the shift in the middle of her note to more positive stroke/traits.*

---

*Here's a case where reading the words wouldn't by themselves convey the strong negative emotion exhibited in the strokes. The writer controlled the written note to avoid alienating her intended reader.

SUBJECT 19

Now is the time for all good
men and women to come to the
aid of their country. And when
I have a million dollars I will

Theodore Hamilton Sellum

SUBJECT 19
TED, CONTROL YOURSELF! – (Ted)

Father was an air base commander, mother was a teacher. They provided love and discipline for their only child who is now a college freshman. He desires to be a golf pro and golf shop owner. Seventy percent of the time he is inclined to be **expressive** and **empathizes** with others (over 60 degrees right slanted upstrokes). Plus he's inclined to be enthusiastic (long t-bars). His adjustment traits; unusually intense efforts at being **cautious** at every turn (long final strokes at word endings); and, even more cautious when family name is on-the-line (see his longer signature finals). Through the years Ted probably heard many comments telling him to be careful about getting into any embarrassing situations that would reflect unfavorably on his father's high position. Perhaps his mother, working in a structured teaching environment, also contributed to his being overly cautious. I bet you he takes a lot of time for his next golf shot!

Diplomacy exercised regularly (note letter sizes receding in words: 'time', 'men', 'come', and 'when', 'million'). His **analytical/investigatory** skills are strong (note m's, n's, v-shape) and his **exploratory** behavior is present in the saw tooth (inverted v's seen in m's and n's) strokes. To complicate matters further, he is **self-conscious** (final hump of m's and n's higher: see 'man', 'and', 'women', 'when' and 'million'). **Pessimism** is present to a significant degree (baseline slanted downward). On the plus side, he handles critique of his performance well. He's not **sensitive-to-criticism** (no loops in t-stems, his work area; and, minor loops in some d-stems, the physical appearance and personality side of him). Ted has an excellent sense of **rhythm** (even spacing letters and words); and good **precision** (formation of letters). His **memory** is excellent (attention to details in dotting i's and crossing t's); his **goals** are all **practical** (t-bars on stems). Good **manual dexterity** is present in his squared r's.

Now let's add up the traits that would enhance his goals of a good golf game and a profitable pro shop business; and those traits that would limit these achievements.

Enhancing Golf Goals	Detracting From Goals
Some caution could help to offset too much impulsiveness.	Impulsiveness
Good Manual dexterity	Pessimism
Good rhythm in the flow of his game.	Self-consciousness
Good memory helps remind him of the lessons for improving.	Too much caution may increase the pressure on his game.
Enthusiasm is valuable when controlled.	Too much enthusiasm or impulsivity can hurt.
Exploratory thinking aids finding new solutions.	
Analytical thinking helps to improve the overall approach to game and business.	
Diplomacy and good manners will endear him to game officials and his spectators.	
Realistic goals are achievable	

Ted is venturing out to leave the security of his family (wide left margin) while having some trepidation about what the future holds (wide right margin); yet, he is out to establish his own identity in a field different from his father or mother. He has the stuff to succeed.

Now is the time for all good men and women to come to the aide of their country

YOUR STAFF

CATHY BEALS

SUBJECTS 20A & B

"Now is the time for all Good men & women to come to the aid of their Country!

Sandra

SUBJECTS 20A and B

SANDRA'S AND CATHY'S CHILDREN

As lead youth coordinator for a Norwegian Cruise Line, Sandra is a "10"!   Great **sense of humor** (bending initial stroke in 'Now'). **Taking life less seriously** (t-bars concave). **Gregarious** (larger size writing). Very quick **understanding** (needlepoints on r's - artistic talent in squared r's). Very **coolheaded** (near vertical strokes under 30 degrees right slanted strokes), helping her to lead her colleagues and youthful charges. They will not feel judged. She has a good sense of **rhythm** (spacing of letters and words), plus excellent **organizational skills** (balanced f-loops). Sandra **attracts others to her** (finals that curl back up toward the left); you can feel her body language beckoning and saying, "come and follow me". A wonderful combination of traits for a youth leader.

Cathy is another cruise line youth staffer. She, like Sandra, has a great **sense of humor** (bending initial stroke in the word 'now'). You can feel the fun and flow of her rounded (**loving**) strokes; the **rhythm** (even space of letters/words); **open-minded** (wide e's), **directness** (no upstrokes in t's), easygoing **diplomacy** (receding letter size in words), room for **many friends** (y-loop in 'country'). Yet, in spite of all of Cathy's open, easy going, loving, generous traits (broad upstroke finals in 'men', 'women', 'the' and 'their') she maintains **poise** (near vertical upstrokes) and is **well organized** to lead the kids.

Notice how Sandra and Cathy have common strokes/traits found in those with an aptitude for leading young people safely to enjoy fun and frolic on cruise ships.

SUBJECT 21
PICKING AN ACCOUNTANT – (Bo)

What Traits Would You Want?

Concentration (very small writing strokes).
Close attention-to-details (doting i's, crossing t's).
Loyalty (rounded i-dots).
Analytical mind (v's seen in m's and n's).
Exploratory thinking (inverted v's in m's and n's).
Rhythm (even spacing between letters/words).
Steady (baseline straight).
Cautious (straight finals 'the', 'come', 'men', 'women', and 'time').
Cool-headed (near vertical upstrokes).
Organized (balance in f-loops).
Persistent (loops in t's).
Independent (short t-stems, although not that short in this case).
Pride (t-stems 2½ x height of case letters).
Realistic goals (all t-bars on stems).
Determination (straight down strokes, see "community" and "country").
Pessimism (baselines slope down).
Quality orientation (wide margins and space between lines, subject doesn't start without knowing he can finish).
No confusion (strokes do not intersect with other strokes of lines above or below).

Without any significant negatives, I have to grade Bo 9.8 on a scale of ten.

Now is the time for all good men and women to come to the aid of the youth in their community and country.

93

APPENDIX – A PRIMER ON PERFORMING HANDWRITING ANALYSIS

A.   Words about some tools and rules used to perform an analysis.

Keep in mind that the purpose of this book is to use extraordinary writing strokes of uncommon subjects to identify many basic or evaluated character traits. I purposely avoided comprehensive and balanced analyses to simplify, for the layman, illustrating what handwriting analysis can reveal. The art and science of weighing the frequency and intensity of numerous traits and their interaction is a complex task for the professional determining the resultant forces and effects on a subject's mental and emotional processes, their forces to achieve, their fears, their defenses, their social traits, and their aptitudes. For the experienced practitioner a meaningful and credible report would combine all the tools and rules and utilize a worksheet to deal with over 100 plus traits.

A thorough analysis can take three to five hours normally using one or more long paragraphs of cursive writing written on different days and include the usual signature of the subject.

The analysis worksheet organizes the different areas being examined. For example: the number of slant strokes and their percentage in each quadrant of emotional **responsiveness**. The mental **processes** including types of thinking (i.e. analytical, exploratory, comprehensive, cumulative, etc) and those traits enhancing thinking ability counteracted with those that impede ability.

IMAGINATION applied and its intensity in the philosophical/theoretical plane (upper zone); and, its influence when loops are present, in the mundane or material area (lower zone).

In the **FORCES TO ACHIEVE** section the worksheet will provide for judging goals from short range (t-bars low) to intermediate, to long range (up the stem), to visionary (t-bars off the stem). Next the **will power** (weight of T-bar and length for endurance). Heavy **pressure** means strong will and energy with longer T-bars showing **enthusiasm**. **DETERMINATION** heavy weight of downstroke, straightness of stroke, and greater depth below baseline mean great determination; whereas, light pressure, curving and short downstroke show limited determination. Next, all of the traits that help achievers and those that detract will be listed to arrive at a judgment of potential for success.

FEARS, DEFENSES, SOCIAL TRAITS and **APTITUDES** will be evaluated on a scale of 1 to 5 or 1 to 10. The margins and spacing allowed all around and within the writing specimen, and their variability, and trends will give the analyst a holistic (or Gestalt) approach to the world as viewed by the subject (generally I review this first). Now you have an outline for a comprehensive balanced handwriting analysis.

APPENDIX B

STROKE DIRECTION (SPACIAL PLANE)

The direction of strokes in the visual plane – their meanings:

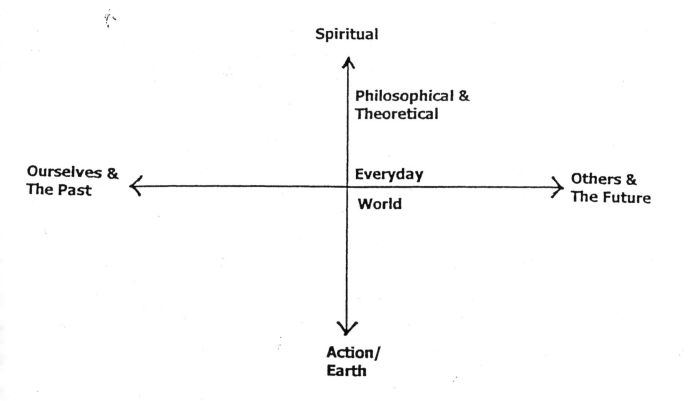

APPENDIX C

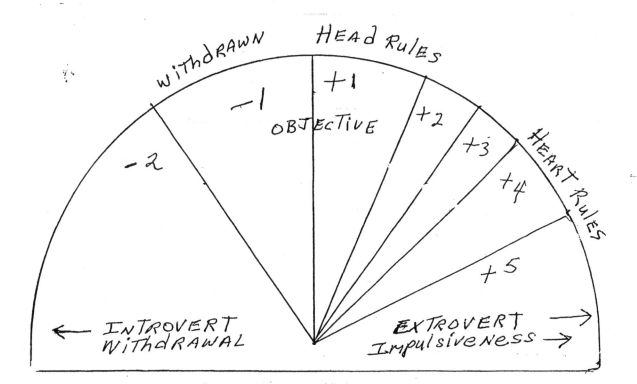

Slant Gauge

Emotional Responsiveness

APPENDIX D

GLOBAL/UNIVERSAL TRAITS

D1 **SLANT MEASUREMENTS:** Responsiveness with others: Far rightward means more impulsive, emotional, from the heart behavior. Near vertical slant – the head rules in decision process and emotional expression limited (others don't feel judged). Left of vertical withdrawal from others emotionally; self-interest security first.

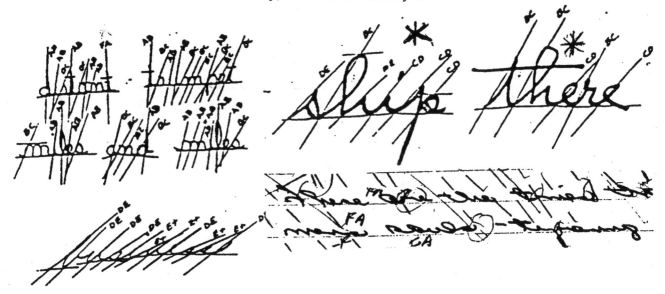

D2 **PRESSURE (DEPTH OF FEELING, SENSORY IMPRESSIONS):** Heavier downward pressure of writing instrument means greater depth or lasting emotional or sensory memories; whereas lighter line pressure writer's memories of experiences fade faster; these writers don't savor the past like the heavy line pressure writers and, light writers are less likely to hold onto resentments. **Medium pressure** writers are not subject to the negatives of heavy or light. The preference for a particular writing implement may be an indicator of a person's depth (i.e. fine, medium or heavy ballpoint).

D3 **SIZE: LARGE STROKE WRITERS:** Generally have higher energy levels; they are individuals who are actively interested in experiencing a wide spectrum of life's opportunities, assuming other traits or physical impediments aren't preventing them from exploration. They are likely to be extroverts. The can be more subject to distractions.

SMALL STROKE WRITERS: Generally are very focused on details. They are inclined to be introverts. They may appear to be anti-social[1]. They make good technical or research workers. They are commonly more conservative and frugal people.

MEDIUM SIZE STROKE WRITERS: Have aspects of small and large writers but with less intensity. Their flexibility and adaptability give balance. Often they are teachers or sales persons.

---

[1]   Keep in mind loved ones and friends will often witness different behavior of a personality than the persona viewed by the public.

D4 **RHYTHM:** Even spacing between letters and words. Often seen in good artists and musicians; business persons with good rhythm are able to accomplish more work.

Now is the time for all good Women to come to the aid of

D5 **IMAGINATION:** (Loops in writing). Wherever loop strokes appear, imagination is evident. The fatter the loops, the greater the imagination.

A. The higher the loop above the baseline, the greater the depth of abstract, theoretical, spiritual imagination experienced.

Sample A.

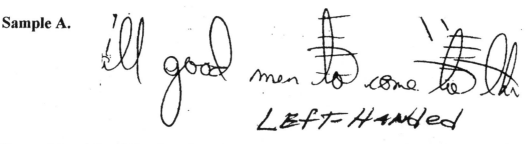

LEFT-HANDED

B. Material or Mundane Imagination: The deeper the downstroke below the line and size of the loop, the greater the amount of imagination. For example, those with deep "y" loops below the baseline have a need to meet more people.

Sample B.

aid of this country

APPENDIX E

SOME RULES FOR OBTAINING VALID SPECIMENS

1. Obtain several samples, preferably cursive writing, written on different days.

2. Ballpoint pen on a pad (or half dozen sheets) of unlined paper to obtain best indication of the downward pressure of writing.

3. Avoid specimen provided knowing it was to analyzed.

4. Be sure specimen was accomplished in writers natural position i.e. not with any obstruction or interference like standing or blocked. This may introduce traits/strokes not representative of writer.

5. Long enough specimen to obtain capitals, many different letters, plenty of t-crossings and I-dots plus variance in margins.

6. Writing about a familiar (loved one) or business subject makes for more natural expression.

7. Have recent specimen(s).

APPENDIX F

SOME STROKES/TRAITS FOUND IN THE LETTER "T"

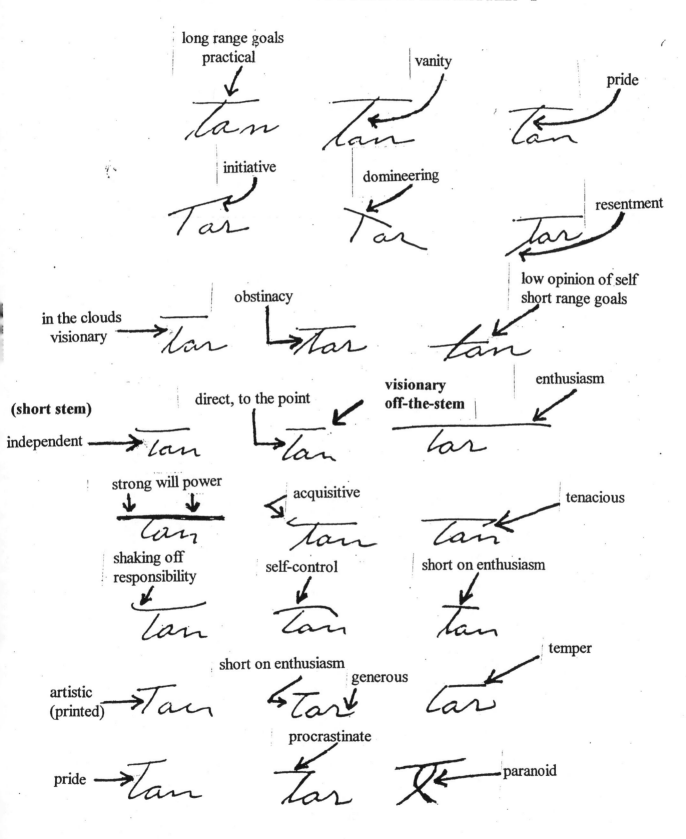

long range goals
practical

vanity

pride

initiative

domineering

resentment

low opinion of self
short range goals

in the clouds
visionary

obstinacy

enthusiasm

(short stem)

direct, to the point

visionary
off-the-stem

independent

strong will power

acquisitive

tenacious

shaking off
responsibility

self-control

short on enthusiasm

artistic
(printed)

short on enthusiasm

generous

temper

procrastinate

pride

paranoid

BIBLIOGRAPHY

Bunker, M. N. So You Want To Get Married, 1953 International Graphoanalysis Society.

De Sainte Colombe, Paul Grapho-Therapeutics – Pen and Pencil Therapy 1966-1972 Devorss & Co.

Dr. Teltscher, Herry O. Handwriting – Revelation of Self Psychographology 1971 Hawthorn Books, Inc.

Green, Jane Nugent You and Your Private I (Personal Pronoun I) 1975 Llewellyn Publications.

Harrison, Phyllis and Don C. Matchan Helping Your Health Through Handwriting 1977 Pyramid Publications

Holder, Robert You Can Analyze Handwriting 1958 Prentice-Hall, Inc.

Lowe, Sheila R. The Complete Idiot's Guide To Handwriting Analysis 1999 Alpha Books

Mahoney Ann Handwriting & Personality 1989 Ivy Books/Ballantine Books

Marley, John Handwriting Analysis Made Easy 1967 Hal Leighton Printing Co. Bancroft & Co.

Marcuse Phd, Irene Guide to Personality Through Your Handwriting 1978 Arco Publishing Co., Inc.

Metzler, Mary, MGA Letters of the Alphabet Analyzed 1981.

Metzler, Mary, MGA Margins Revised Edition 1981.

Morgan, Chris Handwriting Analysis 1992 A Quintet BookSmithmark Publishers, Inc.

Nadall, Florey Pen In Hand 1965 Doubleday & Co.

Olyanova, Nadia, <u>The Psychology of Handwriting</u> 1973 Wilshire Book Co. <u>Handwriting Tells</u> 1969 Bell Publishing Co.

Page, Eileen, MGA <u>A Positive Approach to Awareness and Understanding</u> 2nd Edition 2000.

Rogers, Vimala <u>Your Handwriting Can Change Your Life</u> 2000 A Fireside Book

Schermann, Rafael <u>The Secrets of Handwriting</u> 1976 Warner Destiny Books

Schram, Geraldine Moore <u>Survival Skills for the Information Age</u> – A Graphoanalytic Approach to Business in the 21st Century 2002 Burnham, Inc. Publishers

Singer, Eric <u>A Manual of Graphology</u> 1969 Crescent Books/Crown Publishers

Solomon, Shirl <u>How To Really Know Yourself Through Handwriting</u> 1973 Bantam Books